EX TRACTION

EX TRACTION

poems by

Lara Coley

Button Publishing Inc.
Minneapolis
2024

EX TRACTION
POETRY
AUTHOR: Lara Coley
COVER DESIGN: Zoe Norvell

Published by Button Poetry
Minneapolis, MN 55418 | http://www.buttonpoetry.com

Manufactured in the United States of America
PRINT ISBN: 978-1-63834-089-8
EBOOK ISBN: 978-1-63834-095-9
AUDIOBOOK ISBN: 978-1-63834-094-2

First printing

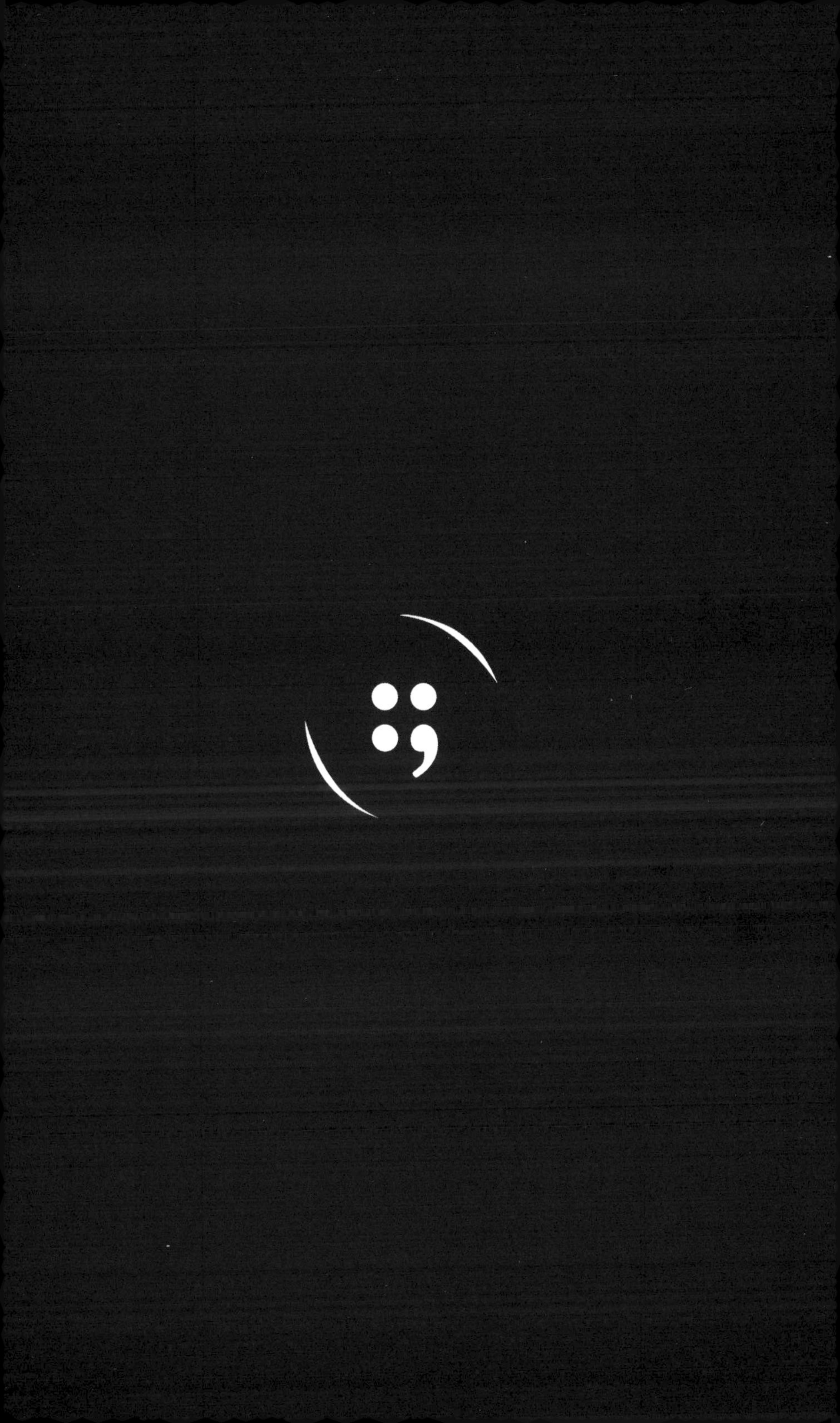

EX TRACTION

Remember that time you did that thing that made me love you even more and when I leaned in to breathe the belief you ripped my teeth out from my expectant lips and scattered them round town like time bombs so that as long as I lived here I could walk down any street and be shattered by a part of my own brokenness?

I do

CONTENTS

1 The Women Who Make Wishes on Their Burning Lashes
2 The Men Who Carry Heavy Shadows
3 Minutes
4 The Women Who Hold Coffee in Their Mouths until It Cools
5 For Clarity's Sake
6 Bait
7 Take My Breath
8 Playing Pretend
9 The Women Who Travel Alone
10 The Ocean Asks Me
11 The Women Who Know Where Bone Meets Bone Is Softest
12 The Women Who Love in Past Tense
13 While It Lasts
15 Ambrosia
16 The Men Who Build Cathedrals in Bedrooms
17 The Men Who Are Cradled by Darkness
18 The Women Who Leave Like Boomerangs
19 Miles and Millimeters
20 The Scale
21 Sugared
22 The Women Who Have No Name for Their Hearts
23 You Punctured My Solitude
24 The Women Who Trade One Poison for Another
25 Hard
26 The Women Who Tend Graves and Call Them Gardens
27 The Men Who Do Not Get What They Need
28 Performative Verbs
30 This Was Your Home
31 Holy Be My Name

32 The Women Who Forget They Know How to Swim
33 The Handle of the Axe
34 How a Name Is Given
35 The Men Who Wear Shadows as Uniforms
36 Lay to Rest
37 The Women Who Have Holes Where Their Stomachs Should Be
38 Eros
39 The Women Who Trace Their Names on Changing Constellations
40 Reclaimed
41 The Women Who Ask Silence to Speak Louder
42 The Hollows Are Everywhere
43 Our Throats
44 Two-Timing
45 The Women Who Strike Matches Under Water
46 Like a Lullaby
47 The Women Who Eat Memories with Their Fingers
48 Patrimony
49 The Women Who Drink Approximations in the Blue Light of Morning
50 The Last Time
51 A Good Fit
52 Combustion
53 Ways to Keep Him
55 Mythologies
56 The Men Who Pick Locks of Open Doors
57 The Metallic Taste of Love
58 She Weighed It in Her Hand
59 The Women Who Only See Their Reflections in Dreams
60 How to Become Meat
61 To Begin With
62 Memento Mori

63 The Men Who Love the Ones That Don't Want Them
64 Bodies Are Always Happening to Us
65 The Women Who Are Buried Breathing
66 My Teeth in Flames
67 No One Has Come Back
68 The Women Who Ask Silence to Speak Louder
69 The Gift
70 The Fruit on the Bough
72 I Am So Tired of Writing about How You Broke My Heart

75 Acknowledgements
79 About the Author
80 Author Book Recommendations

EX TRACTION

THE WOMEN WHO MAKE WISHES ON THEIR BURNING LASHES

You light the body on fire before you're finished because you need a reason to walk away. Walk is not the right verb for moving backwards from the sputtering blaze. We forget that doors don't let the light in, cages do. What if a kiss is a cage? What if a mouth is nothing but teeth sharpened in the dark, crooked with the way you chew your dreams in sleep? They ask for more of me, less of your tongue, your lips and skin. But it's the space between the bars that holds the tiger. Is that the right cliché? I mean to say, I am the body on fire. I mean to say, I am ash, I am bone, but I was flame. I drank the goddamned gasoline.

THE MEN WHO CARRY HEAVY SHADOWS

You are disappearing into the shadows of the past. Not to say that you'll be gone but I won't see you for all the darkness made by obstacles that once were, and the ever-tiring speed of love. This mangled heart, scars still stinging, ghosts clawing for the rights to this smile or that touch. What flesh is left untilled for you to plant a stake? I am in love with volumes, never the mass. Potential is luminous. Your disappointments are already well weighed. Every night I look up at the stars, I hear you whispering, *It's a graveyard of suns.* Imagine what the graveyard of loves looks like. Imagine how it must shine.

MINUTES

This is happiness.
This is how long awe lasts
This is the number of times you can kiss before you start losing
This is the phone call
This is the time it takes to drink nervousness
This is your weight in patience
This is the muscle your breath flexes
This is your thumb casually hooked in a heart
  like the top of a pair of faded jeans
This is the gravity of a freckle
This is red rushing warm
This is how you paint the face of places that matter to you
This is the kind of undressed that blossoms skin
This is the substance that fills us when beauty takes breath away
This is our mouths aching and the feeling that wells before a laugh
This is how long you can touch without learning to juggle
This is the number of *no*s you should say before *yes*
This is the taste of sunrise
This is a hotel bed
This is the bed we sweat in
This is my heart looking for something you said
  when I was under your arm in a bed in another country
This is kindness stacked and dealt
This is the question you did not ask
This is a receding horizon where the word *love* should be
This is how to find the center of home
This is how you hold something that does not fit in your hand
This, remember, is happiness.

THE WOMEN WHO
HOLD COFFEE IN THEIR MOUTHS UNTIL IT COOLS

I am making my home a den of missing. I want more space to hang pictures of me in your head so I take planes and trains and make space into distance. Synonyms aren't the same in translation. Gentle comes out quiet, it comes out soft. These are close but they're not you. Home looks like steam with your hands wrapped around it, keeping the heat in. My heart used to crumble in hands like that, but it grew steel skin. I bash it against lips, throw it at ribcages. The bruises aren't mine. I can say *I love you* in six languages but the tongues curdle, so I spit out your heart, *ton coeur,* where no one can hear. Here. This place I call home.

FOR CLARITY'S SAKE

I'm not chewing the syllables,
they won't digest.
I know the food on the plate
won't satiate,
I'mgonnaeatitallanyway.
Every sound in my body says
not the one
but he says things plainly
and I like the way they sit
clear
on the table when he sets them down.
The expectation
is the hurdle.
The expectation is the knife.

BAIT

The proximity of pleasure ravages the room. The devil is in the details, and by details, I mean, the things I want to do to you. This is where I should swallow my spark, hold back my sweat and panting, contain my sizzling skin because pretty girls waste themselves on empty words and that emptiness weighs like lead on a line. Two fingers fit in this mouth just as well as any hook, so hold me up like the lured feast I'll become. Take all the pictures you want. We're not allowed to touch but let's make a list of all the *shouldn't* things we've done or want to. Tell me I'm pretty and I'll bite first.

TAKE MY BREATH

I will never love the way I'm supposed to. Like splitting the wishbone still in the flesh, you know I want to leave you, so before I get the words out, you put me against the wall, knot my hair in your fists, rip away my resolve like a wave that unbreaks, moving backwards out to sea. You look at me like meteor, like storm, like lightning striking the same exact place every time our mouths meet. You are calm and unquestioning. You are all muscle and bone and teeth. You are stone and wall and silence on fire. How do you love so softly, so gently, so quietly, with your hand so tightly cradled around my throat?

PLAYING PRETEND

It was like children
playing tea.
I poured you tiny teacups
of nothing
and you drank them in
gushed over the delicacy,
the sweetness.
You savored the warmth
till I began to believe
we were eating cakes,
little heavenly cakes.
You rubbed your belly and laughed.
I played along,
marveled at your fullness,
waiting for you to notice
the voids you swallowed,
to throw the tea set to the ground.
But you spread your smile
and asked for more.

I didn't love you.
I was pretending.

Like children playing tea.

THE WOMEN WHO TRAVEL ALONE

I don't mind the weight of carrying clothes, water, journal on my back. Mountains rise and skies bloom under crumbling shoulders, but I can't carry the weight of men's eyes as I pass alone like I'm a doe bleeding on a plain, or how *que linda!* is said like a groping hand, or the way everyone asks, *you travel alone?* as if danger lies in my body moving through the street. *Claro,* I answer, even after I meet him, and we share meals and buses and rooms together. The man at the hotel desk asks if I feel safer now, with this man, who's shorter than I, speaks no Spanish, who lost his watch and wallet, drunk in clubs. *No,* I answer, *but he probably does.*

THE OCEAN ASKS ME

to stop drowning myself and swim, every smile on the surface, a boat home. Let's watch them sink while I drink you away. The legs on this wine look sturdy and there are bottles enough. I'm spooning out my insides and choking on details. You think I'm trying to forget but what I mean is, there are colors in the sky we've never seen together and I plan on swallowing them like the sea, like the sweat I licked, flat-tongued from your back. We won't feel like we lost anything but we did. You say waves break to rebuild like we're the sea, regathering. But something is cracking underneath us. Hear it? Something so thin, it sounds like the fall of dreams, waking the moment they touch the ground, but haven't shattered yet.

THE WOMEN WHO KNOW WHERE BONE MEETS BONE IS SOFTEST

I have written you so many times, sometimes you become the words and the flex of my hands. Remember how I loved your hands? No. You knew to interrupt before those words got out. I am so filled with your stories that I want to call your dad and ask him how his head is feeling and if he still hides my letters to you from her. I am feeling better since you left, since I beat you to leaving. Waking up alone is not like dying or moving to Italy, but somewhere in between. I am still in love with the midpoint, the crook of your elbow, the cup of softness as you stirred, pulling in and letting go. The give. I am still looking for more of that.

THE WOMEN WHO LOVE IN PAST TENSE

He died on a new motorcycle on his twenty-fourth birthday. When I was that age, and he, nineteen, we made love in the Italian countryside during a Christmas snowstorm. The trains stopped and I stayed in his bed for days. He was in love with loving well and he moved softly, carefully. Took his time making meals, lit the stove with gathered wood, poured Italian wine and French compliments between kisses. *Why don't you love me like I love you?* he asked me in English. I wanted to say, *The years between us are filled with lessons and I see too many shadows where you see light,* but answered instead, *It'll make sense when you're my age. Find me then.*

WHILE IT LASTS

A button on your shirt is missing.
If I didn't wear armor,
if I wasn't wearing gloves,
I would have said, *just there,*
your heart and you would have seen
the stark nakedness you carry around.

But I don't. I want what you have,
so I take your mouth,
your hands, press them
on me, let them leave marks.
You call this desire, but
avarice pools like blood
where your teeth promised *soft*.

Your hand around the back of my neck
loosens,
levels us
in letting go.

I wake up tender
swelling in the smell of you.
I'm not taking any words off the table
but you brush *sorry* away,
say, *bite me here.*

I can't say why
the pull
the claw
the choke.
I can't say why
such sweetness either.

While you're cinching your belt,
while you're calling a car, I ask,
Why won't you?
You say, *I will. You just wait.*

AMBROSIA

You smell like liquor, like you spent the weekend in Vegas with cool droplets on a glass keeping your fingers wet. You have me needing you before your lips meet mine. I'm always hungry and you feed me whatever I ask for, I'm tempted to ask for seconds, for hundredths, for *never-leave-your-bed-again*s. I begin to hate my skin for not touching all of you all at once, every freckle and tan line like a map to a memory I won't make if I don't take you in fast enough. I don't know how to lick to the center—I say *lick* but I leave a bruise. You have only ten fingers and I am counting on them to knead me into something like the mouth of an ocean. Salt spills into my hollows and my hair tangles into something like a nest. You settle in. I wake up to the sound of your breathing and I know that's the sound of space being made inside you and disappearing again, stirring again into a low hum of hunger. Your fingers slip in the sweat along my spine and tiny exhalations build like condensation on the skin of your neck. You are all flex and pull, smooth and warm. I drink you in like liquor.

THE MEN WHO BUILD CATHEDRALS IN BEDROOMS

No one thinks they're starting a religion defending what they love. Your heart was an abandoned chapel in the mountains and my lips were holy like mercy, like water to thirst. Remember when I was sick two months, lost thirty pounds, could barely walk, and some guy in the park loudly told his friend I wasn't worth fucking from behind with that skinny little ass? You poured kisses on my body like honey and cream, and I put the weight back on with the hunger you had for me. You fed me till my curves filled my clothes again, then you prayed to them like you were a religious man, a god-fearing man, a man that believed in heaven.

THE MEN WHO ARE CRADLED BY DARKNESS

Your monster of a mother doesn't know how to open her arms so you practice aiming lower. When she gets cancer, you think she planted it herself to prove a martyred point, but when she gives you her car, the terror hits you like a bus. You're used to being driven very carefully and now you are in charge, it is you who could kill all the fragile animals on the path. You turn off all music and silence the things you've always longed to hear. You focus on the dark. You slip quietly into it and the words, *I love you,* become no louder than a nod. Your heart gets still, so still, it may have even stopped, but how would anyone ever know?

THE WOMEN WHO LEAVE LIKE BOOMERANGS

The first time he dumped me was the morning I noticed how sunlight made him look like love. The second time was after I slept on the couch at his friend's house, his friend I'd had sex with when we were broken up. The third time, I knocked on his door, car packed to go camping but only silence answered. The fourth time, after the party where he danced with his ex-girlfriend, Jessica. He hated dancing. The fifth time was my turn. We were lying on my bed and I asked him why, in our two years together, he'd never told me he loved me. He said he didn't need to, that everyone knew. *Even Jessica knows,* he said. *Well, good for her,* I said. *Good for Jessica.*

MILES AND MILLIMETERS

You get points for something good but I forget what. Maybe it's for believing something when you said it, for not knowing the difference between what you said and what you felt, for being so sure of your precision, *I love you a tonne and I mean metric.* I wish you'd had better things to say, given me something substantive to measure. No one speaks the same language. We say the same words but there is no calibration of the weights we tie to the heavy vowels in *us,* in *love,* in *gone.* A man in the town I'm from went to buy ice cream during a rain storm and a mountain cliff slid onto his home and his wife and his two tiny sons while he was waiting in line. There was the same distance from the store to his house that night. The same syllables in the word *driveway,* that once ended at a door and then, a pile of stone. The same tonnage of tree when it slipped from where it grew to land exactly where his bedroom had been left with the light on. We try to forget distances and we hold bodies close, wrap them around us. We forget that while one is measuring the distance *to,* the other is measuring the distance *from,* and both fit in the precise sound of something thundering down, very far away, ringing in our ears, and yet, silent, like mountains in our mouths.

THE SCALE

I stop eating meat because I still haven't found the right body under all these pages of magazines, the undercut of women saying, *you're so skinny,* as a compliment, and the skin scratching itself as it grows and contracts under the wishes of others' hands. I'm losing mass. He tells me I'm losing the fullness he craves. I tell him to close his eyes and pretend then, but he says, *No, I want to look at your bones, the hollows of your cheeks. You are becoming a beautiful ghost.* I've lost my spine to some carving away of hope. I only love him because I can pretend he chose the wrong word for the terrible thing he's saying, can pretend the accent made me hear beauty in the dark he's making, can hear my dearest songs smothered in different places in his throat. Those lullabies buried me sometime before my body became my own, so asking for another's permission feels like paying respect, *a family tradition.* This is the sentimental compost I've made of us. Look how cleanly I've piled the bones in this meat, letting you wrap me in newspaper ads, slicing where lines say prime and chuck, weighing me warily, like a butcher. One that can't stand the feel of the flesh that's in his hands.

SUGARED

God is winking like a high-class hooker.
He plucks the stain off my lips,
calls it a kiss and says, *Doesn't it feel like*
peeling a beating heart with your teeth?
He thinks there's something left to taste in me,
dips his finger into my throat
and fishes out the sugar like I'm a cold cup of tea.
He's licking his nails, knuckles, wrist,
but this honey is to his elbows.
I want to ask him where he found the sweet
when I can barely make the salt of sweat,
but his eyes become mine, suddenly green and blue.
To love yourself is to know god, he whispers
but I only want to know what his mouth tastes like.
God's eyes are my eyes and
he says, *here, take me in your mouth*
and call me any name you like,
so I unclench my angry jaw
and he stitches my tongue with thistle.
The blood tastes sweet, like lava
before you know it burns, like love,
before you know it leaves.

THE WOMEN WHO HAVE NO NAME FOR THEIR HEARTS

When I feel nothing, you're there, and seeing you there doesn't change the nothing into love. It reminds me of The Never-Ending Story, the Rockbiter holding out his empty hands. I imagine leaving, the sense of sadness you'll feel, saying with upturned palms, *They look like big, strong hands, don't they?* Everyone will nod, not knowing what to say, you make it seem so immense, the loss, this love swallowed by a storm. We dissolved like a dream you can't remember but you feel haunting you for months. You're still holding on, still searching for a name to call into the night, a name to give the fading spark. But there's nothing left to hold onto, no matter how strong you are.

YOU PUNCTURED MY SOLITUDE

Like the give of a cherry,
split with longing,
the inextricable sweetness of tearing
to get to the heart.

No, that metaphor is not enough.
We crack like ice put to flame,
ride our own melt
till the body's bulk is gone.

Still. No. It's another song,
or bird. The moon's reflection
on a bottle or a broken tooth.
What if I said you were the beginning
and the end? A flight.
A fall. But no.
The knife.
You are always the knife.

The way you slip in,
sharp surprise that enters
easily, cleaves a slice,
and is gone,

your absence staining,
remaining in the toughness of flesh
that comes with scars,
that covers tender seed of separation,
sweet
and red as cherries.

THE WOMEN WHO TRADE ONE POISON FOR ANOTHER

Some nights, you sat upstairs watching those girls undress and dress, shades open, from the bedroom window while the rest of us played a game of kings downstairs. I think of that now when I find porn open on his computer and hope he won't touch me tonight. You used to touch me those nights the same as the nights you were downstairs drinking with us, which is to say, very well. That time on the river when you traded your hat to see *some hot girl's tits,* I asked if she wanted you. You said she probably thought you were a dirtbag, *but it was a real good hat.* I laughed. You were so goddamned sexy, I just laughed.

HARD

I pity the girls on the bus,
the young ones, all angles
and straight yellow hair.
I know what they want:
curves, supple and round.
And they will get them.
No longer will they stick out their ribs
to mimic soft slopes of breasts.
They will wake up women,
round and full,
begin to wish for angles,
to run every day,
thinking always,
it was so easy
when they were young.

THE WOMEN WHO
TEND GRAVES AND CALL THEM GARDENS

We visited Normandy, le Point-du-Hoc, a beach where you can still see carved scars of battle, empty bunkers and a bombed-out base. A cemetery. A tank. I think *indestructible,* then I think how many ways I can take that word apart and start humming the tune to London Bridge, *we all fall down.* I can't find a word for the way I want to wrap myself around wrecked bodies, a word for the embrace of a car around a tree, pieces not in pieces but still not whole, or the dark cradles that explosions build, how they hold the bodies we once held, and the bodies lie waiting to unpack their bones. Not gone, not fading, but entirely
undone.

THE MEN WHO DO NOT GET WHAT THEY NEED

He said he dreamt of me in Thailand. He hadn't slept in days. His bed was full of teeth and he'd scratch before he'd wake. Then one night, I came to him, led him out on the sand, and in silence we looked at the sea. When he tried to speak, I kissed him, a blue light filling our mouths, filling his lungs. It flooded him with something like the moon melting on his tongue. He woke up and it was morning, but he still felt an opal glow in his throat, the air of the sea on his skin. He carried the light inside him, carried the cerulean heat in his chest. When he tells me, I say, *That's what my love feels like,* but he shakes his head, *I don't think this is something I can feel every day.*

PERFORMATIVE VERBS

You couldn't say the words
because words stain, because
they're remembered, they get written down.

You couldn't say the words
because they were needed
and you like holding what someone needs
out of reach, close to you,
on the inside pocket like a checkbook,
like a promise unbroken but unkept too.

You couldn't say the words
because they're like holding a bird tight,
knowing the smallest shift means finish
or flight. You couldn't say the words
because you liked to cradle
that choice in your hands.

You couldn't say the words
because they're so easy to say
when you mean them,
and even easier when you don't.

You couldn't say the words
because they looked like roots,
like kindling and smoke
like god and home and the sweat after sex
like rain-stained cathedral ceilings and thunder
and like the ocean underneath you and the sky above and

you couldn't say the words
because they looked, up close,
like a color you never knew had a name,
a name you'd never said aloud before.

You couldn't say the words
because they looked like everything
and nothing at all.

You couldn't say the words
because you'd heard them, said them,
choked them up and filled buckets with them,
you'd bailed them, frantic,
out of so many sinking ships.

You couldn't say the words
because they were soft
and you liked the cold of metal,
the smell of stone.

You couldn't say the words
because they did not save you then,
and they will not save us now.

THIS WAS YOUR HOME

Out my window and a decade after,
a light is on in your building and I remember
all the ways I said, *I love you,*
but never meant, *in love.*
The division is wide. Do you remember
the ways we knew to say nothing
and fill the spaces between us?
                                                        I was not
good to you. I left so much of you
before I left you, let so much of you down.
Worse, I never missed you,
not the way you looked or spoke,
your green eyes or your smooth palms,
not the places that were once ours
or the ones we wanted to be.
But I'm standing at my window,
your old room has the light on,
and I can't turn a memory off,
the one where we stood at your window
looked out
                        and believed
that this city was ours, believed we could
be each other's home.

HOLY BE MY NAME

I want to be in the dark places. Where you go looking for a word you've forgotten, I want my name to scratch through instead. When you're angry at your boss and you want to scream into the void of his flaccid face, I want the elevator to echo with galloping damnations in my name. And when you're thinking of your ex and that thing she used to do to you that you liked, *so much,* I want you to imagine that, but where her name should be swimming, the letters of my name come floating to your tastebuds instead. And now, as you see the depth of my smiling dimple as the indirect proportion of the distance between my heart and yours, I want to feel my name written in the fissures as your brittle walls crumble, and the dust, I want the dust so full of my name that you choke when you try to whisper that maybe, just maybe,

I might be expecting too much.

THE WOMEN WHO FORGET THEY KNOW HOW TO SWIM

I loved him but if he continued to disappear as he had for the last fifty days, there would be nothing left of him in two months, and when I arrived in Paris, it would be to make love to a perfect stranger who would love me for the very moments that were slipping from my skin like translucent, shimmering drops when stepping out of a pool. Wringing my hair of its heaviness, the cool snakes of him fall from me, slithering away as I forget the feeling of swimming in him, the feeling of him over all of me at once and his eyes, the clear green pools I'd drowned in. Or blue. I could have been drowning in blue pools, now that I think about it.

THE HANDLE OF THE AXE

is made of wood.
My body cut
of the same felled flesh.
The force of needs
returning
like history,
like teeth at flesh
again
and again.
Blade on body,
body holding blade.
This
is the way I will love you.
This
is the way I've been loved.

HOW A NAME IS GIVEN

It comes down to the difficulty of dividing difficulty into parts. If it were only your back and the smooth stretch of muscle, if it were easy to say, *this is what pumps the blood, this is the blood, this is what makes the blood run,* and set them on the table. But the mess is sticky, it smells sweet, tastes salty. It's another inextricability to count when I say *knife* and you see desire. But let's look at the blade, the smooth-to-sharp like the break of a window before it falls. Sudden, and not at all. This is to say, if you are in the poem, then the space between your teeth is as slick and menacing as the man in a bar, *right here.* I say, *if I keep writing love, it still exists.* The man smiles and slides a hand up my thigh, *what a sad synesthesia you sleep with,* he says, hoping that's not what I'll sleep with tonight.

THE MEN WHO WEAR SHADOWS AS UNIFORMS

Long after I left you and you became what you became, I heard about the deaths, about the men who ripped open your city, who lit metal into bone, who wanted to spill blood from bodies like yours, in the neighborhood you patrol, in the one where I said, *I feel safe here, no matter what they say.* I searched the photos online for a glimpse of you, feeling ridiculous for looking at asses of heavily armored men, for thinking I could identify you by only that, that I know you that well, every inch of you, the sway of your walk, the line of your hair, that I even know the way cloth touches you, how you want it close, want it to feel like skin, how you want it to hold you together.

LAY TO REST

Look at the careful way you love,
hand on softness, mouth licked clean
and ready. You are mine and I
am monster. *What part of me do you love?*
You beg. *Name it. Give me a word, a sound,*
a refuge.
I refuse,
and you dig for love to chew on.
You dig like you believe what's buried
is breathing,
like you can hear its voice,
like it's something you can still save.

THE WOMEN WHO HAVE HOLES WHERE THEIR STOMACHS SHOULD BE

You brought me something dark and steaming to wake me up but I don't drink desire plain. Milk and sugar. Cream and molasses. I need some goddamned sustenance. You were hiding in your lackluster darkness and I want someone to love like he's starving, bruising all the fruit in his hunger, all teeth and blaze. You rely on the kind of electricity that requires switches. I need the shock of lightning and the boom of its heartbeat, the kind of light that rockets across the backs of my eyes, heaving shuddering sparks. I want to be fucked till I'm filled with sky, to be left clawing at the moonlight, swallowing the stars.

EROS

I string hearts
like pearls,
wear them cynically
to weddings.
I wash myself
with soft, sticky nights,
make bodies my bathtubs.
Tongues and fingertips
scrub my skin,
salvation
in hot licks of saliva.
I dress in silks and dew
but catch my myself
in fogged bar mirrors
wearing nothing
but want.

THE WOMEN WHO TRACE THEIR NAMES ON CHANGING CONSTELLATIONS

You say *steady* low and calm because it's what we say to keep a horse from kicking. But it's not a word for the waves of affection we gather and release like tides. Not tides. Lightning. The way beauty strikes itself then disappears. How can we carry such darkness and stay light? We watch the ocean spliced into pitch and moon and sometimes we feel so full with magic, we hear hearts cracking open and we know to let go, to brace for bruise. We know we can see a star fall from the sky and not lose a thing, so steady are we.

RECLAIMED

He becomes a stone in my belly, then a fist, then a war, and still, I swallow and say it's better this way. I can't build the stairs out of here because the only instrument I can find is the hammer that broke me and I won't let that touch me again. He asks, *explain your scars one more time, I want to see the knife more clearly,* but I think he likes to peel open my skin and see what bleeding looks like on my naked body. He likes to see my hair pulled tight and hold no responsibility in his hands. He says, *I just want to save you and I don't know how,* but I see the blade. I know he'd slice through me just to count the rings, just to see where there were fires and say, *I never burned you like that,* pointing to rings of ashen pasts, covered in sawdust he's made of cutting me down.

THE WOMEN WHO ASK SILENCE TO SPEAK LOUDER

It is very easy to ruin and very difficult to maintain. One could argue that these make the same point but we argue about smaller issues, about how the words *j'éteins* and *je t'aime* sound the same with your sleepy Southern accent, and how, when I say, *je te deteste*, it means you break my heart with every silence that comes after love, silences so pure, I start to hear a violence in homonyms. We live entirely in our mouths, tongues beating each other, kneading each other into softness, into stone. I should have learned to enunciate, to move more carefully around the sharpness of your words. The space between your teeth is as close as you ever got to love.

THE HOLLOWS ARE EVERYWHERE

Fill them.

Take your hand,
here. Your mouth.
Take me in your teeth,
release. Pull kisses

and a handful of hair.
Look me in the eye.
Don't stop.
Look me in the eye.

Listen to the quiet thrum
of blood and hunger.
Listen to the whimper,
the rummed honey.

You are smooth medicine
and I will swallow every spoonful
you spill in my mouth.

OUR THROATS

are raw. We don't know
from which fire anymore, which
fight. Ash tastes like something
we don't know is lost till it rains on us.
I tear my photos up, fill my
bowl with milk, chew my lover's
childhood, swallow
like a smoldering storm. Gone.
How many ways to let go.
Someone is standing next to smoke,
counting. Someone is making a sound
so thick with sobs, it erases
the screen door squeal
forever. The well-fed
can't understand hunger,
and we cannot understand
how good the mess in the sink
until we stand shocked
by our sink in the mess.

TWO-TIMING

you’re splitting me
not breaking
that would be easy
pieces to hand out
like candy
and I wouldn’t feel so selfish
to have this heart
so ripe and ready
it aches
to give you
thick slices of me
dripping like peaches
in your warm hands

THE WOMEN WHO STRIKE MATCHES UNDER WATER

It is not only that you sucked out my dreams and chewed on them like soggy toothpicks. It's that I can't remember the last time I really wanted to fuck you. I can't remember if I ever did. You forget the important thing, which is I was the best you could get and you are the most good I will ever have. It's funny how little those are for glue. When you made promises, I believed them. You gave your kindness so quietly, I listened harder, tried to hear more, but I tired of your *yes yes yes,* that same saccharine every day, like the perfume that exploded in my bag, making me sick with its sweetness. I finally understood *too much of a good thing.*

LIKE A LULLABY

You're not generating lies when you're kissing,
so muffle my meaning with your tongue, lift me like a ship.
Be ocean, be crash and heave and wet caress.
Don't think of your children, sleeping cotton soft,
don't let my skin shine smooth and white
like a moon you can't reach. My hands
can't make the orbit around the arms you carry,
the weight of names you say goodnight to.
When my breathing smooths, let me go,
wave goodbye into my hair, my palms, the crepuscule of lips
and teeth and tongue, here in the night, firmly fit
into the muscles of my mouth
and yours. Hush us,
hush us
before good intentions escape.

THE WOMEN WHO EAT MEMORIES WITH THEIR FINGERS

When it falls apart, I trace my skin like I'm still the feast you said I was. I say words like peaches, honey, and rum, but I feel the crack of the shell that spills me out of myself. I remember the way you made eggs, leaving one side untouched—smooth—while you burnt the other side solid, so it could only be ripped apart with a blade. I remember how, when we were alone, you'd slap the back of me so hard, welts bloomed like dandelions on a lawn, quick and everywhere. Then you'd meet me in the street, kiss my face so soft that girls looked at us with eyes of hunger, whispering, *what I'd give for that kind of love*. I try to forget what I did give, what I wouldn't give again.

PATRIMONY

I told him I started gaining weight after the election, my body filling with fear. He asks who could I be afraid of—they don't all come to mind at first, but for days after, I think of the young men, young white men, rich with unearned indemnity. One who held a knife to my throat while his friends laughed, one who stood outside the door while his friend finished, one at a party who slipped into my boyfriend's bed with my passed-out body when my boyfriend made a run for beer. I don't tell him about the ways my body was unsafe with people who look and talk just like him, but when he says, *well, he isn't president anymore,* with an instructive nod towards my thick thighs, I see I'm still using men like him as mirrors to cut myself with.

THE WOMEN WHO DRINK APPROXIMATIONS IN THE BLUE LIGHT OF MORNING

I lost something. I wish I knew what it was so I could look in the last place I had it. I wish the remedies of the past could make something warm again. I would fuck the fire back into me if I could, or drink it in burning gulps of whisky. I would learn the back of someone's hungry hands like a country and follow them home if it would do any good. I would love something if I could find a thing I didn't see the cracks in. But there is a brokenness waiting in everything, a wreck in everyone who ever loved, and I have been mapping the rifts since the day you wouldn't say you love me. Everything has been falling but you.

THE LAST TIME

Most times, you don't know it's happening.
I used to make love after goodbye,
to savor their smell, to forgive
the things I never could before.

There's a coldness in having no words left,
but having only words weighs heavy
in a mouth not kissed.
These teeth have been missing you,
have had nothing but sibilants
between them, have not split a skin
but peach's, and we know that fragile flesh
puts up no fight, tears like paper wet
with saliva and a light touch.

I want to hold the pleasant lie of endings,
the fire of autumn leaves
becoming
a dry and tender gold,
smelling sweet
and fresh
but dying.

A GOOD FIT

She is wearing your affection
like a coat, tailored
to fit her.
I remember stretching your love
around my shoulders
like a misshapen shawl
that would never cover any parts of me
that needed warmth.

COMBUSTION

In Rome, we visited ruins, awed by a permanence we would never be a part of. Look at the faces we made in photos, I'm good at playing happy, at writing a script for the flush in my chest and putting on the mask. You liked the stage where heroes bow, splashed in blood and valor. Do you remember the night you waited angry in the rain, followed me into my building and vibrated rage into the gripped arm of my coat, how you would not let go? Did you know what was in my mouth? His sweat and promises. When you stripped for bed in the sweltering hotel room, you tore your clothes from your skin, laughing, but I saw a beast's form in the ragged edges of cloth, a yellow flicker in your cat eyes. This is to say: *I loved you*. You never hid the darkness, and now, I smear the black of coal over me, call any licking a flame, beg sparks for their crackle, snap my bones to hear your voice in the silence of my room. Since you, I dig through everything ravaged and beautiful for something to light on fire, for something precious to ruin.

WAYS TO KEEP HIM

Remember the details he numbered
and named, *good,*
how he made them shine.
Remember that the speed of light means
your face is already dying
in the eyes that hold you.
Remember that the color of the ocean is always
a reflection of something else.

So if it means alone,
bend, bow,
just don't *break.*

Remember when you were done faking,
wrenched and moaning like Christ came
back, how he'd sometimes recline
on his knees, sanguine, looking like a man
you could love, how you thought,
this must be what god looks like
when god believes in himself.

If it means alone,
open, wet like peeled
lemon, sprinkle sugar where it stings.

Remember that drought can come after rain,
and flood can come after drought,
that you used to be beautiful
when you had a heart uncharted
like a wide country inside you.

Remember how war was waged
for details, for *the way*
the words were said.

If it means alone,
stay
small.

MYTHOLOGIES

If I made him a god,
I could forgive, could
call his salacious hunger,
desire, his penchant for bruise,
lust. I could call him the knife
because blade to flesh is
meat, blade to meat is
sustenance, and something
in the beating makes me
tender, makes me easy to
chew. That's what he liked,
taste of destruction
as element of seduction.
Took the map of home
from my bones, carved
a monument of losses, braided
hope of morning into unkept promise
of night, cast the rest to sea,
let lesser gods break pieces,
take pieces of me.

THE MEN WHO PICK LOCKS OF OPEN DOORS

The last weekend you came to visit, I asked you not to. You never listened so I said goodbye in every conversation and cafe. On Sunday, you said it was the longest you'd ever spent with me and not seen me naked. I stood and stripped. I turned in front of you, slapped your hands away, and leaned in, lips to your ear. I whispered, *voilà,* and kissed you, then began to dress again. I'd read your text to the other girl. You always said you knew you'd get hurt, you were so sure I'd stray. Come closer, *mon amour,* listen *de près*—it was always you throwing rocks up in the air, waiting to blame gravity for the bruises on your face.

THE METALLIC TASTE OF LOVE

If you and I were wounds on a body,
I would say, *Look,*
this is where we enter.
You would say, *Watch,*
the exit will bleed.

Everything important is either flesh
or metal. My language or yours.
You asked how I would kill you.
You said, *Just for fun.*

In bed, I replied. *I'd kiss you real soft*
and press the knife you gave me
gently into your chest. You smiled,
said, *I never did like nice girls,* looking proud.

The best way to survive is to leave.
Don't stay in a pot that's boiling.
Don't stand in front of a moving train.

I've carried your love like a knife lodged
deep in my own gaping chest,
always measuring the risk of losing blood.

You may be the thing that kills me.
You may be the thing keeping me alive.

SHE WEIGHED IT IN HER HAND

It was like nothing, the way you put women into and out of flames like chops on the bone, the same way I used to say *I love you* in foreign languages. *Amour* is just a word for a word, not a proper feeling. But you? I'll say your name to anyone who asks, I'll draw out your phonemes until they look like notes released by piano's teeth. You say you're a different kind of kindling and the smoke around you smells lemon fresh, so I hold back and my desire slips into a dress called shame. I point to the music and say, *Look at the way the white contains nothing but still holds it all in place. Look at the way violence spills into silence.* Any city can be burnt to the ground. Ruins are beautiful until you become one, smoking at the ends of your fingertips, trails of ashen hair. Look at the hooks hanging from the mouth of the floating fish. Someone calls that an art. Tell me where your animal body's hiding and there will be acres of psalms that rhyme with you. Give me a shovel and under what tree your heart. I'll dig. I'll dig, I'll dance, I'll do what you ask. Catching your love is a maneuver as tricky as playing musical chairs to your most beloved song. The circling, the pull of a body that wants to stay moving, the knowing the words so well, you still hear them even when the music's

cut.

THE WOMEN WHO ONLY SEE THEIR REFLECTIONS IN DREAMS

I split my lip on the cracking facade when I kissed you, started to see the two-way mirrors, the way you watched without letting me in. If you were fruit, you'd be a bitter one, with thick, sweet-smelling skin, one I'd have to dig my nails in deep to get to the juice. Is it possible that one break makes broken but two makes whole? When I say break, I mean wild horses. When you say love, you mean in pieces. You carry everything so carefully while I ask, *This, love, why can't you hold onto this? This is the one that will flee if the gate is left open.* You say, *Then that is not the one we want.*

HOW TO BECOME MEAT

I always start with the knife. Handle made of the bone exposed as the buck grows more and more male. The blade shines like that night that Mars was so close, you said my lips shone red like berries or blood. You made us a bed in the wild dark, splashed with some small flower I'll never know the color of. The grass beneath us was dying, which I know because it fell from my hair on the winding drive home and filled the backseat with gold, dry and brittle. You called me so often, I stopped wanting to be wanted, stopped seeing planets approaching as extraordinary events. I don't remember your last name, but I remember your girlfriend leaving you sitting at the bar, the sharp tone she said goodbye with. I can't imagine now what she thought the first time you talked to me, the way you watched me as I walked away, while I carried a cold beer from the bar you sat at and slipped it onto the table of another man, counting change while your eyes nibbled at my fingertips. I was still beautiful then. I had a way that was envied, some kind of spark and smolder. She probably found someone better, better than a man who said, *marry me,* as we lay damp and glowing in the light of uninhabitable planets, just days after she left him, just weeks after I saw him for the first time as I brought him a steak and asked, *do you need a knife with that or are you going to tear it apart like an animal?*

TO BEGIN WITH

I handed him a strand of hair,
he twirled it between his fingers
and marveled at the shine.
I pulled them out,
plucked each silky wisp for him,
one by one.
He kept misplacing them.

I gave him my eyes
smooth and blue and white.
He rolled them round his palm,
kissed them for luck,
and lost them in a game of marbles.

I gave him my heart
warm, red mess
heaped in his hands.
He held it to his lips,
sucked it dry,
let the shriveled mass slip
and fall to the floor.

Nothing left to give
I asked for it back,
for it all back.

He shrugged,

I never asked for any of it
to begin with.

MEMENTO MORI

This will end, is what you tell yourself, your eyes spilling into your ears while he keeps pumping, thrusting like fleshy machinery, driving air out of your barren chest. You are flipping through lovers like a rolodex to try make your sounds sound real because your voice is empty and you're sure a sob is coming unless you can find a face to replace this man's, as he tries to make you love him like he loves you, tries to make you look at him like you're hungry. You're getting fat from wanting anything but him. You're getting mean from saying *no* when you want, so badly, to want to say *yes*. You should leave. You should leave before your name is etched into your ribs in his voice. You should leave before you lose the thing that makes you think you know how to love. You should leave, and you picture it, picture putting on your clothes, telling him goodbye, and never having him heave and sweat on top of you again. You think of this as he hangs a limp arm over you, and the thought glows orange, sparkling, hot like the head of the match,

about to burn the whole house down.

THE MEN WHO
LOVE THE ONES THAT DON'T WANT THEM

When I heard you'd cheated, I let myself forget how fast I'd called him when we broke up, dialing his number as I walked from your car, tears still drying on your face. When I saw you at the restaurant a couple weeks later, sitting at the table next to mine, I hoped you'd heard every word I'd said about him. I hoped you'd heard how heavy his name sounded in my throat, the gratified purr my voice became because he'd been inside me. After dinner that night, you left a message that you'd always be a little in love with me, that I looked beautiful, *ever always beautiful*. I tell our story and you're the monster, the heartless liar, the untrue. But we both know who did what to whom.

BODIES ARE ALWAYS HAPPENING TO US

And they never stop happening.
I made of a list of muscles that were mine,
the selection of salts I've melted between tongue and skin,
but all I want is to sink my teeth into a heart
that will break them in half.
A rock to stand on,
to weigh me down for once, to keep
me from floating in some far-off tide,
from leaving myself again and again.
The bodies keep coming
and I say *skin, hands, lips, soft,*
but I claw and dig for more,
for just one look
underneath,
at what holds them steady,
one taste
of what makes them strong.

THE WOMEN WHO ARE BURIED BREATHING

I know how the story ends. I've slept with every color eye and when I spark, I smell the ash in the air. Every bird of love and butterfly and creature that could flutter by, anything that sings or that I told you I believed in, was caged and beaten purple while it sang a song of living. The silence, my dearest, is deafening. The sound of walls remaining in their place. Of hardening cement. You, lover of music and maker of noise. You have made the thud of heaving brick onto brick sound like a heartbeat. No, you have done the reverse. You have made the act of making love sound like stone settling on stone.

MY TEETH IN FLAMES

My tongue used to be pink with desire,
wet on whiskey, weakened on wit.
There used to be taut brown
muscle to clean, black eyes groping,
and the scent of sweat under my nails.
I used to bury men in bitten lips, leave
trails of four dug in rippled backs,
crosshatched like street maps,
handprints that hummed,
you lucky son-of-a-bitch.
I used to light house fires
and whistle in the crack, split, pop
of want.
    But *you.*
                You looked at the ash
on my fingertips, said,
Here, if you like heat, take a sip.
You filled my mouth with gasoline,
turned away when I kissed the spark.

and told us how it feels to be the one after. I was ravenous for a man who could fill me after you and I ripped open the chest of the first sturdy one, ate him with a spoon. He knew me best, he knew me worst. Imagine a man who's had paths dug into his back on every continent but could never follow you anywhere but away. I would sometimes go back to my room after walking him to the door and there was nothing of him anywhere. I liked it. I never wondered how you felt when the girl after me left you, if you held onto details of her to fill the spaces with. I know the holes I dug in you. I know where your bones were soft with bending the truth and the weight of the lies you filled yourself up with, thinking they built you strong. I knew they were going to drown you, but you wanted to believe, so I let you believe with someone else, and let you bring her down with you instead.

THE WOMEN WHO ASK SILENCE TO SPEAK LOUDER

The days have turned suddenly cold and the consistent might of melancholy is a fog that lives somewhere in the filter of my eyes, just under my skin, like the layer of milk when you boil it. The sticky film that divides liquid, warm and corporal, from vapor, clinging to the chill on windows. Your hand on my face, in my hair, gone. But what is on my tongue if not you, what is the word I want to say if not, *drowning*? I know how many times I said, *stay,* the same number you left. I know what I look like pleading in poem after poem, but bitterness comes in spoonfuls doled out by people so close, I just open my mouth and say *ahhhhh.*

THE GIFT

There is blood on the knife but you lick it clean. I notice you have no scars, that your bruises heal before they become any color that's not beautiful. Mine are rotten greens, appear like freckles in the sun, *easy.* You turn the blade over in your hand, find a new way of looking at it every time you slide it out of my skin. Nobody believes it's my fault because, *look at this mess you left.* No one runs at a knife more than once, do they? Your eyebrows dance at the question and the way my fingers finger each scar, like a sleeping baby's hand, delicate and small as a milk drop. You say, *you hold your pain in reverence.* I say,

give me something else to hold.

THE FRUIT ON THE BOUGH

The lime blossoms litter and bloom.
Because I am lost, I think of the sky, the shifts of heaven
that spread themselves into our photographs,
the long stretch of Normandy monuments.
Someone imagines the colors pale and soft, tearing
the darkness from the drowning, the sigh
from lungs of exhaled halos.
A becoming, then a fade.

I think of the limes ripening,
of all of the springs I've plucked,
the sunsets I carry.
I think of the blossoms burying the earth,
the confetti of petals. I think of the tongues
I've ripped souls from, the heavens
I've breathed out for nothing more
than warm hands. I think of love,
how it breaks. How everything does.
Dawn. Sleep. Silence
into song. A fall. The speed
at which we live.

Because the jasmine continues climbing,
I think of you. The way your eyes
wrapped around me, around the smallest curves.
I think of the skin on your shoulders,
the flecks of sunny days,
the weight of kisses I lost there
again and again.

I think of your hands on a piano,
the songs you played that made the weather.
I drown in the beauties that ripen without you,
without me. Because I've been missing everything
since my senses went smoky,
since my all hope went dark.

The flowering fruit dreams of sweetness,
of satiated thirsts. How many
hearts can you hold in a fist, how many mouths?
Look at the plaster, it crumbles. The bed
is burning. The skin blossoms.
Somewhere in the orchard something falls silent.
Somewhere, she is peeled.
There is always a question of wanting.
The sky, holding light like a child.
The sky, spilling stars like handfuls of sand.

I AM SO TIRED OF WRITING ABOUT HOW YOU BROKE MY HEART

They say strangling takes strength, as does letting go. You watch a light leave from up close. I want your lips on my skin to say goodbye, I want to feel the words form in your throat, under the fragile bones of my fingers. Your breath's vibrations are already filling my lungs with absence. Your silence is syrup I choke down like medicine. When I say medicine, I mean numb. I mean cold. I mean *goddamn I miss your voice when there are these seas between us.* Then you lean close and whisper, *that is just a jar of tears, no sea.* I know. *I know.* I'm just so tired, all this nothing breaking my heart.

button
poetry

ACKNOWLEDGEMENTS

An enormous thank you to Button for publishing voices I'm so very honored to be part of. Thank you for being truly good to us.

I am incredibly grateful to the editors of the following publications that published the poems listed (some in a different form):

Love is the Drug and Other Dark Poems
"EXTRACTION" & "EROS"

Rogue Agent
"THE GIFT" as "Un Cadeau, Un Couteau"

New American Writing
"THE WOMEN WHO ARE BURIED BREATHING" &
"THE WOMEN WHO FORGET THEY KNOW HOW TO SWIM"
as "The Women Who Forget There Is Water"

Quiet Lightning
"THE MEN WHO WEAR SHADOWS AS UNIFORMS" as "St Denis"

The League For Innovation
"TO BEGIN WITH"

Denali
"TWO-TIMING" & "TO BEGIN WITH"

Thank you to reading series Red Light Lit, Quiet Lightning, VelRo, The Racket, & others for allowing me to read with exceptional poets.

DeYoung Museum, for inviting me to read some of these poems in the same hall I'd listened to my heroes read in growing up.

You were generous and kind to me.

Thank you.

WITH PERSONAL THANKS AND GRATITUDE

My adopted sisters, I may have written a book but I don't have words to capture what you mean to me & the ways your love sustains me:

Big K, you are my anchor & inspiration & sitting with you feels like home. Wendy, you revived me with your heart, brilliance, hiwawity, & your gift for making everyday moments magic. Brook, thank you for believing in me more than I often did & reminding me to go for eff yeses. Dana, you are the funniest, most generous writer I know & you keep me sane. Sophia, who weathered it with me. Jesse, thank you for your wisdom, always delivered with sharp humor & a soft touch. Love you.

Jon, Tim, Sam, Anita, Lorette, Niall, Kim, & Roz, you each saved my soul at some point & you probably don't know it.

Jennifer & Red Light Lit, this book (& a good deal of my confidence on page & stage) would not exist without you.

Fisayo & Lisa, for sharing your genius so generously. I see you in my best poems & I love you as people as much as I admire your work. Lots.

VelRo dads, Gavin, Fisayo, & Presley, you bring the best tears. Austin, Jenny, Dirk, Sofia, Kacy, Kar, Loria, Matt, Keith, Daniela, Kim, you are what makes writing life good. The Poetry Center's gracious Elise & Steve, for making our band of bleeding hearts feel at home.

The OG CWs, Dana, Briana, & Brandon, you talented beasts.

Mentors Carolina, Toni, & Jennifer, who modeled the community building, magical writing & fierce gentleness I aspire to. Thank you for loudly believing in me and my writing. Babs & Imagining the Book, this book exists grâce à vous. Dan, who told me that I would "make it as a poet" until I believed it. Sparks, who made me send my first poems.

Andrew, Maxine, Paul, Mario, Chanan, Truong, Matthew, Nona, Barbara, & SFSU Creative Writing Department. You inspire daily.

Goli, Kim, Arlette, Jen & Meghan, the kind coaches in my head.

For sharing your hearths and hearts: The Eldridges, Donna & Amanda, Jen, Wendy & Willy, Roxy & Mike, Martine, SJ & Mark, Anna, Emma & Gui, La, Autie, Lola & Roseline. Renata & Alex, for the example, the love, & making me a floof auntie.

Jen, Francisco, Megan, & Mario, thank you for many years of support. You are more like family than bosses—I love you like miracle pancakes.

Ma famille française, Martine & les gars, Anaïs & Romain, Ann, Marie, Roseline, Gaëlle, Maya, Emma, Arida, Yvette, Caro & Thomas, Tom, & Alison. Je vous aime, mes biches!

The fabulous, kind, talented, brilliant, loving, hilarious humans who have supported or inspired me in ways too many to name: Will, Allen, Gui, Nate, Jake, Jeff, Henri, Antoine, Allyson, Nicole, Neval, Maggie, Brad, Kayla, Tongo, Miah, Steph, Sasha, Ellen, Jen, Evan, Preeti, Danielle, Jacob, Léa, Sarah Fran, Nick, Patsy, Ploi, Leslie, Anna, Katie, Diana, Yonny, Josh, Santos, Jesus, Diego, Basi, Jose, Victor, Matt, Aiden, Poot, Luci, Miguel, Brian, Jack, Adam, Suhail, Christine, Servando, Gimer, Paco, Israel, Hraban, Hendrick, Alex, Heather, Mason, Eva, Chay, Teo, Max, Solange, Rae, Ren, Juli, Steve, Andrea, Emily, Aimee, Chris, Renee, Rachel, Molly, Tiffany, Scott, Mack, Andy, Andee, Grace, Sam, Sally, Autie, & many more. Merci.

Holly, who shared the books that formed my love for reading. WWW, the best witch in the west & the most blessed. Dida & my large, loca family, who make art, sing, dance, laugh & close that front door with great gusto. Amo! My mom, who made sure creativity filled our home. Grandpa Russ, Karen, & Connie, who took over & took care.

Ruth Asawa School of the Arts & Heather, for having me as an Artist-in-Residence, working with the most caring & talented young writers.

Please forgive me if your name isn't here. The number of people who have supported & inspired me & my writing over the years overwhelms me when I try to express my gratitude in words. I feel incredibly lucky & loved.

ABOUT THE AUTHOR

Lara is a San Francisco poet and educator with an MFA from SFSU. She has taught creative writing and ESL in juvenile detentions centers, high schools, universities, and mental health treatment centers, and has worked as a reading series curator, poetry editor, editor-in-chief, content writer, fellow artist-in-residence, coordinator for the Poet in the City program, and server. She is the recipient of awards including the Browning Society Dramatic Monologue Prize, the Daniel J Langton Poetry Prize, the League for Innovation Poetry Prize, and service awards for supporting underserved writing communities. Lara's work is featured in journals including *New American Writing, Visible Ink, Rogue Agent, Red Light Lit, Opium Magazine, Transfer,* and others.

She currently lives in the South of France, working as an English teacher and somatic self-development coach while studying marriage and family therapy.

AUTHOR BOOK RECOMMENDATIONS

Ain't Never Not Been Black by Javon Johnson

Johnson's *Ain't Never Been Not Black* reminded me what poetry can accomplish in making us feel what we have not experienced ourselves. This book FILLED me with feelings. Johnson quickly introduces us to the themes of celebrating Black community, strength, and beauty, the racism that tries to tear them down, and the well-merited anger that can come with being Black in racist America. By the end of the third poem, "Near Death," I am angry right alongside him—and in awe of his talent. So precise in the depictions of injustices, the poems take the air from my lungs and fill them with fire.

Butcher by Natasha T. Miller

Natasha Miller's *Butcher* is dauntless. A portrait of bodies that are unsafe for how they look and who they love. Intimately personal and universally devastating. The metaphors are powerful, built by the veracity of the language and clarity of the images. Miller distills inhabitable moments of suffering, of triumph, of courage in the face of hate and, sometimes as frightening, love. *Butcher* depicts the ties between joy and pain, feelings that too often come hand in hand, especially when Black and queer in America. A must read.

Swallowtail by Brenna Twohy

Twohy writes bravely and beautifully into scars and secrets. *Swallowtail* lets us be destroyed—and rebuilt—with each poem. I felt her haunting, visceral descriptions with my whole body. Twohy's metaphors are so masterful, I wrote down the ones I love most and had two full pages—I can't stop rereading them, despite the ache they carve into me. "Grief is not a feeling/but a neighborhood.//this is where I come from./everyone I love still lives there." Anyone who has struggled through loss or trauma will feel this book in their bones.

OTHER BOOKS BY BUTTON POETRY

If you enjoyed this book, please consider checking out some of our others, below. Readers like you allow us to keep broadcasting and publishing. Thank you!

Desireé Dallagiacomo, *SINK*
Dave Harris, *Patricide*
Michael Lee, *The Only Worlds We Know*
Raych Jackson, *Even the Saints Audition*
Brenna Twohy, *Swallowtail*
Porsha Olayiwola, *i shimmer sometimes, too*
Jared Singer, *Forgive Yourself These Tiny Acts of Self-Destruction*
Adam Falkner, *The Willies*
George Abraham, *Birthright*
Omar Holmon, *We Were All Someone Else Yesterday*
Rachel Wiley, *Fat Girl Finishing School*
Bianca Phipps, *crown noble*
Natasha T. Miller, *Butcher*
Kevin Kantor, *Please Come Off-Book*
Ollie Schminkey, *Dead Dad Jokes*
Reagan Myers, *Afterwards*
L.E. Bowman, *What I Learned From the Trees*
Patrick Roche, *A Socially Acceptable Breakdown*
Rachel Wiley, *Revenge Body*
Ebony Stewart, *BloodFresh*
Ebony Stewart, *Home.Girl.Hood.*
Kyle Tran Mhyre, *Not A Lot of Reasons to Sing, but Enough*
Steven Willis, *A Peculiar People*
Topaz Winters, *So, Stranger*
Darius Simpson, *Never Catch Me*
Blythe Baird, *Sweet, Young, & Worried*
Siaara Freeman, *Urbanshee*
Robert Wood Lynn, *How to Maintain Eye Contact*
Junious 'Jay' Ward, *Composition*
Usman Hameedi, *Staying Right Here*
Sean Patrick Mulroy, *Hated for the Gods*
Sierra DeMulder, *Ephemera*
Taylor Mali, *Poetry By Chance*
Matt Coonan, *Toy Gun*
Matt Mason, *Rock Stars*
Miya Coleman, *Cottonmouth*
Ty Chapman, *Tartarus*

Available at buttonpoetry.com/shop and more!

FORTHCOMING BOOKS BY BUTTON POETRY

Neil Hilborn, *The Future: Limited Edition*
DeShara Suggs-Joe, *If My Flowers Bloom*
Edythe Rodriguez, *We, the Spirits*
FreeQuency, *On |(Un-)Becoming*
Ollie Schminkey, *Where I Dry The Flowers*
Topaz Winters, *Portrait of my Body as a Crime I'm Still Committing, Special Edition*

Available at buttonpoetry.com/shop and more!